DARK PSYCHOLOGY
AND MANIPULATION

*Learn the Most Effective Manipulation &
Brainwashing Techniques to Protect Yourself
from Manipulation and Analyze People with
The Art of Persuasion & Mind Control*

Written by:
Patrick Norwood

Table of Contents

PATRICK NORWOOD

Introduction

Among the fundamental human rights, freedom is for every living being to have opinions, points of view, perception, and perhaps a say to every matter that arises. Forcefully taking away this right from individuals is an unfair and inhuman act, and is therefore against the law in many nations of the world. But then, people still tamper with others' perceptions; manipulate people's minds for diverse reasons without applying force. This is called "The Psychological Manipulation" and of course, not a crime.

The ability to manipulate minds is indeed a great gift, skill, and a great possession to any and every human. In fact, it is fun to manipulate minds, but not in any way funny to be manipulated. As the manipulated, you may feel emotionally bullied, you may sense cheating or develop a kind of inferiority complex towards the manipulator, but you don't have to negate this psychological skill and art of manipulation, all you need to do is to be on a safer side by learning about the art of manipulation.

Not only the power embedded in the possession of the skill, but the results to be gotten from the effective utilization of this gift is enough to paint psychological manipulation as one thing that a goal-oriented and smart person must possess. Psychological manipulation is basically about getting into people's subconscious, reading minds, getting people to do what you want them to do (believing you, performing an action, making or taking a decision, accepting your stand on an argument, confessing, obeying an authority, following an instruction...). In this case, not with force but by convincing them and making them see the reason to do what you need them to do. It is basically being smart psychologically and using it to achieve your aim. It is your ability to study, persuade, influence, and manipulate minds and get people to be on your side irrespective of their initial stand or characteristic. With this said so far, it'll be pertinent to present a detailed, relatable and realistic example of how manipulation works.

There was a time when one of my cousins would always get me to agree with him on whatever we were discussing or arguing about. He was so good that I couldn't win an argument even with my clearly valid points that were better than his. What I know he had was that he knew how to make me agree with him. Even when I tried to prove smart, he was apparently smarter. He could control my mind through persuasion and not force. Like magic, he would always know what I was thinking about, hence, he could easily counter my thoughts and propositions. He had studied me well and his psychological manipulation was prime. But as time went on, I got to realize that being able to get people to reason with you, be on your side, change their perceptions or get yours to fit with theirs, win arguments and get into their minds isn't magic after all. It was and still is a matter of being smart and using your smartness to its fullest capacity: psychological manipulation. Studying people, reading minds, observing people and situations, taking advantage of circumstances, watching more and talking less, and doing lots of critical thinking are other ways of getting to be a controller of minds, a psychological manipulator, and a very persuasive and influential individual.

Does any idea of manipulation come lurking in your head yet? Are you able to visualize any incidence or a potential incidence of manipulation you've ever come across? Do you feel so elated now because you've realized that you have subconsciously used the psychological manipulation power on someone before? Or you fall into the "I don't even have any idea of what you're saying" category? Don't worry, whatever your category, this book is here for you. But before we move into the business, let's create a little image.

Another relatable example or experience we might have had with manipulation is the manipulation that is contained in the power of persuasion through brand's PR (Public Relation) officers and marketers while they provide you with messages that capture your attention, sustain your interest, create impressions on you and sometimes even influence your perceptions and/or purchase decisions. Persuasion and manipulation happen even on the streets; getting to be convinced by a saleswoman at the nearby grocery store about patronizing her store. Another example is when your mom would buy you a storybook then instead of a toy, and was able to convince you to understand why you needed the book and not the toy. It is used by a cheating lover when they try to erase their cheating record from your mind and slowly drift the blame away from themselves and unto you.

Can you relate it to those your neighbors who are persistently encouraging and persuading you to come to their social or cultural group? When you're influenced and convinced into visiting the library every day or drinking every other day because you've been conditioned to do so owing to the manipulative abilities of your peer. So, you see that the "playing with minds" and the persuasion thing is a chain with endless rings. Would you keep being the manipulated? I doubt your answer is yes. This is the book made for you to read with all the concentration and interest in the world. You've likely grabbed a copy though for you; however, there's one more thing, read up! Soon enough, you will learn to control minds and have the necessary persuasive effects of a good mind controller. While getting an insight into what this book is all about, you'll get to understand that manipulation is not evil after all, it's a rather effective use of smartness, sound intellect, and persuasive abilities. Read on!

CHAPTER 1:

What Is Dark Psychology?

D ark psychology is often defined as the study of a human condition relating to the psychological nature of humans to prey on others. Humans have the potential of victimizing others as well as living creatures. Although some people will exercise restraint, others act on their impulses. Thus, dark psychology tries to understand the perceptions, feelings, and thoughts that result in predatory human behavior. Unfortunately, for most people, you never really know that someone is preying on you until it's almost too late. Dark psychology makes an attempt at understanding the perceptions, feelings, thoughts as well as subjective processing systems that result in predatory behavior that is antithetical to the modern-day understanding of human behavior.

It's assumed that 99.99% of the time the motivation behind dark psychology is rational, purposive, and goal-oriented. This means that dark psychology is always present in the world as many people use tactics such as lying, persuasion, withholding love, and manipulation to get what they want. In most instances, these tactics are successful because they can read your mind. Thus, you can choose to either remain ignorant, live in denial, and risk being a victim, or learn how you can protect yourself from psychological exploitation. When you understand the principles and ideas behind dark psychology, you will be better prepared to protect yourself from manipulation.

Although a majority of people have a consciousness of wrong and right, you need to keep in mind that a dogmatic approach to life alone fails to recognize how humans naturally behave, and this will certainly make room for them to fall prey to others. Over the years, philosophers and psychologists have been trying to explore the reasons why people do bad things to each other. A common observation is that people have the capacity to malign, something they're unlikely to do when acting individualistically. Alfred Adler, a medical doctor from Vienna who while introducing individual psychology, holds that human beings are often motivated to act by individualistic approaches to the world. These experiences and approaches could be motivated by imprinted experiences that are inculcated early in life, like an inferiority complex.

This approach perceives human behavior as being purposive and says that human beings only act based on intentional and purposeful motivations. Even then, we can't be blind to the fact that it's silent to the extent to which behaviors, imprinted early in life, influence our way of acting, making a person's actions to be non-purposeful. If anything, practitioners of dark psychology will imprint or program their victims so that they're able to control and manipulate them. They teach you to trust them and even follow them by exposing you to cues and signals that instill these feelings and beliefs. A good example is someone who sends you mixed signals of both distance and closeness or hate and love. The fact that human beings are able to form powerful emotional connections with other people can only mean that you must be on the guard lest you find yourself easily manipulated. The bottom-line is human motivations of dark psychology can be either unconscious or purposeful.

CHAPTER 2:

Differences Between Persuasion and Manipulation

Many people fail to recognize the nuances between manipulation and persuasion. Despite the fact that both seek to convince someone to do something, they are quite different in enough key ways to be classified completely differently. One is only beneficial to the manipulator (manipulation), while the other, ideally, should benefit both people (persuasion). Because of these key differences, manipulation becomes far more insidious than persuasion. The manipulator sees the other person as a tool, a means to an end, whereas the persuader sees the other person as a partner.

Defining Persuasion

Though persuasion involves changing someone else's mind, it is not necessarily a bad thing—there are plenty of ways that persuasion can be used innocently or benevolently. Persuasion is any method that will actively change the thoughts, emotions, actions, or attitudes of another person toward another person or thing. It can be done inwardly toward oneself by changing one's own attitudes or being done to other people.

Usually, persuasion is used as a form of influence—it is everywhere. It is present in ads, politics, schools, professions, and just about everywhere you could think of. If you can think of something, chances are there is some sort of persuasive layer to it somewhere and somehow.

When persuading someone, four key elements must be present. These four elements are:

1. Someone who is doing the persuading.
2. The message or the persuasion.
3. A target recipient for the persuasion.
4. A context that the persuasion is received.

Each of these four key elements must be present for something to be considered persuasive. Of course, this means that manipulation would fall within the category of persuasion as well.

Defining Manipulation

In psychology, manipulation is a type of influence or persuasion, but unlike regular persuasion, manipulation is covert, deceptive, or underhanded. This means that, unlike regular persuasion, which seeks to be most honest, manipulation is often untrustworthy. The manipulator will have no concern about lying about the situation or attempting to coerce the target into believing something, so long as they get what they want.

The manipulator seeks only to serve themselves further, they do not care about the target and do not care about hurting the target. The target is seen as little more than collateral damage; a necessary sacrifice to get the desired results. As such, manipulation tactics are often quite exploitative and almost always meant to be insidious and harmful.

Successful manipulation requires three key concepts to happen. These three are:

1. Concealing the intentions and behaviors while remaining friendly upfront.
2. Understanding the ways, the victim or target is vulnerable and using those vulnerabilities to the advantage of the manipulator.
3. Being ruthless enough to not care about the harm caused to the victim.

Manipulation can take several different forms, but most of them follow the pattern of being covert, harmful, and causing no guilt to the manipulator.

Key Differences

Ultimately, persuasion and manipulation are quite similar: they are both forms of social influence, but that is where the similarities end. While persuasion is generally positive, even within dark psychology, manipulation is not. Manipulation is harmful, ruthless, and insidious in every way, shape, and form.

When you are trying to choose whether something is manipulative or persuasive, there are a few questions you can ask yourself to decide. This simple test can allow you to analyze what you are doing and say to ensure that you are making the best choices for you. If you are not looking to manipulate but the questions tell you that you are erring on the manipulation side, you know to tone it down a bit, lightening up on the manipulative factors. These questions are:

- What is the intention that has led you to feel the need to convince the other person of something?
- Are you truthful about your intention and the process?
- How does this benefit the other person?

The persuader is going to be attempting to convince the other person from a good place—they intend to help the other person somehow. While they may benefit too, they are primarily looking out for the other person's best interest. For example, you may try to convince someone to buy a specific car because it will work better for their family than the person currently looking at it. This would be seen as persuasion, you are offering facts about the other car and showing how it would likely serve the person longer and better.

On the other hand, the manipulator is not concerned with the other person's needs, the manipulator is going to attempt to push for whatever benefits them the most. There is no good intention, and there will likely not be much truth either. It is also not likely to benefit the other person in any way and may even be detrimental. For example, the manipulator may try to sell a car that is no good for the buyer simply because the other car may be worth more money and therefore net a much higher commission. The car is not likely to be very good for what the buyer needs, but that is not the manipulator's concern. The manipulator would see that as something the buyer should know on their own and not bother pointing out the ways that the buyer may be making a bad decision, even if the manipulator knows the decision was wrong.

CHAPTER 3:

Main Manipulation Techniques

We all manipulate people and situations at various points of our lives, like telling a white lie to save our skin or using flattery to make someone like us. For some people, however, manipulation is a way of life and a weapon they use to overpower their victims. Sociopaths, psychopaths, narcissists, and other social predators are critical users of manipulation. While the predators may have a range of techniques with which to overpower their victims, they only target particular personalities. This is because they aim to manipulate quickly and easily, having established the specific vulnerabilities in a person that could render them ripe for manipulation. People with low self-esteem, naivety, low self-confidence, and people-pleasers are quickly manipulated.

Manipulation Techniques

Being able to manipulate someone's thoughts is actually not as difficult as you may suspect, and it can have a powerful effect on your ability to get them to think in the way that you want them to think so that you can have your desired outcome. There are seven ways that people can manipulate others. Unlike persuasion, these are not techniques that you use necessarily in conversation, such as anchoring or pacing. Rather, these are other important techniques that are involved in the relationship you build with the people you are talking to, and how you can use that relationship to manipulate them to have certain thoughts and decisions that work in your favor. The following strategies are an important part of the manipulation.

Trust

Having the trust of the people you are talking to is important. When people trust you, they are much more likely actually to listen to you. They will feel more compelled to have conversations with you, they will be more likely to respect what you say, and they will be more likely to agree with you or comply with you when you exercise authority.

Gaining trust in your relationship comes from using tactics such as mirroring, as well as by generally being trustworthy. Show that you genuinely care about what they are saying and that you have an interest in their wellbeing. Make them feel as though they can feel confident in your ability to think for their better interest, so that they don't have to when they are with you. This way, when you make a request, suggestion, or subliminal command, they are much more likely to comply because they know you think with their best interest at heart.

Cause

You have to have a cause when you are using any type of manipulation strategy. This means that you have a good reason for why someone should do something. When you have a cause or reason why they would want to or should want to do anything, they are much more likely to actually want to do it. The incredible thing about manipulation and mindset is that you don't actually need to have an extremely great cause. As long as the cause is something that can be perceived as important and relevant, you can use it and it will work!

Secret Hypnosis

Secretly hypnotizing people without them knowing it is a powerful form of manipulation. Technically, you achieve this by using persuasion techniques such as pacing and anchoring. The reason why we mention this under the manipulation position is that it is important and relevant in both strategies. If you want to be able to successfully persuade and manipulate people to do what you want them to do, you need to be able to hypnotize them secretly. This is also relevant and important for deception and, particularly, subliminal messages.

When you have people under secret hypnosis, you can speak directly to their subconscious. You don't have to worry about their conscious mind getting in the way. While you do still need to accommodate their conscious mind in the conversation, you have a direct passage to their subconscious mind to help activate your mind control strategies. It is important to understand how important this process is and activate it in every conversation when you want to be in control.

Using Irrelevant Tactics to Accomplish Relevant Goals

Perhaps you have heard of this technique before, but one of the best ways to get someone to say "yes" to what you actually want them to say yes to is first to get them to say "yes" to anything. Often, you want to start by getting them to say yes to things that are seemingly irrelevant to the overall picture. For example, if you want them to buy a TV, you might first get them to say "yes" by asking them if they are interested in having a more luxurious living room or a more comfortable space for entertaining. That way you can then naturally draw them towards a TV and get them saying "yes" about larger sales.

You can also use this technique in many other areas. You can use it to get people to go on a date with you, to get them to go somewhere with you, to get them to give you things, or do any other number of things you might want them to do. This manipulation strategy really puts you in control and helps you get what you want. Soon, you will be able to get them to say "yes" to things that are unbelievably huge for them.

Using Their Feelings

Arguing with logic can be hard because most people are driven by feelings, not logic. Even if they are highly logical people, they are more likely to be driven by logic and emotions, not merely logic. That is why getting into their emotional state and using their feelings to get desired results is often the best way to get what you want.

Proof of Results

People have always been more likely to act when there is proof that the results are what they are looking for. This is why having proof of the results they can expect when doing what you say will be extremely helpful in getting your way. Think about it this way: humans are herd animals; we do not like to be left behind or feel as though we are the odd one out. If you have proof that others have done it, then the people you are talking to are going to want to be one of those people, too. They will not want to be left out or feel as though they are the only ones not doing it, so they will naturally feel infinitely more inclined because they want to follow the herd.

Authority

People are naturally more inclined to comply with someone who speaks and acts with authority instead of someone who appears to be intimidated or uncertain about what they are saying. If you are uncertain, waiver in your stance, or otherwise appear to be under-confident, people are going to pick up on this and will feel less compelled to listen to you. They do not like to follow those who are not confident and strong. This could potentially lead them into a situation they don't want to be in. However, if you are leading with authority through confidence, strength, and certainty, people are going to assume that you know what you are talking about and they will feel more inclined to listen and comply.

Manipulation works heavily through knowing how to assert yourself in a conversation and use a human's nature against them. By understanding how people naturally behave, act, and think, you can use this to your advantage and create a situation that will allow you to carry the control in the conversation and manipulate people's thoughts and feelings to work in your favor.

CHAPTER 4:

Brain Washing

What Is Brainwashing

Brainwashing is basically the process of conniving someone to give up beliefs they had in the past to take on new ideas and values. There are many ways this can be done even though not all of them are considered bad. For instance, if you're from an African country and then move to America, you're often forced to change your values and ideals to fit in with the new culture and environment you're in.

Many people have misunderstandings of what is brainwashing. Some people have more paranoid ideas about the practice, including mind control devices sponsored by the government, which are thought to be easily turned on as a remote control. On the other hand, some skeptics don't believe brainwashing is possible at all and lie to anyone who claims it has happened. Most of the brainwashing practice will land in the middle of these two ideas somewhere.

During brainwashing practice, the subject will be persuaded by a combination of different tactics to change their beliefs about something. During this process, there is not only one approach that can be used, so it can be difficult to put the practice in a clean little box. The subject will mostly be separated from all the things they know. From there they will be broken down into an emotional state that makes them vulnerable prior to the introduction of new concepts. As this new information is absorbed by the subject, they will be rewarded for expressing thoughts and thoughts that go with these new thoughts. The rewarding is what is going to be used to reinforce the on-going brainwashing.

Brainwashing is not a new thing for society. These techniques have been used by people for a long time. Those who were prisoners of wars, for example, were often broken down in a historical context before being persuaded to change sides. Some of these most successful cases would turn the inmate into a very fervent convert to the new side. In the beginning, these practices were very new and would often be enforced depending on who was in charge. The brainwashing term has been developed over time and some more techniques have been introduced to make the practice more universal. The newer techniques would rely on the psychology field as many of those ideas were used to demonstrate how persuasive people could change their minds.

The brainwashing process is accompanied by many steps. It's not something that's just going to happen to you as you go down the street and talk to someone you've just met. First of all, one of the main requirements that come with successful brainwashing is to keep the subject isolated. If the subject can be around other people and influences, they will learn how to think as an individual and there will be no brainwashing at all.

Once the subject is isolated, they will go through a process of breaking down their own self. They're told all the things they know are wrong and they're made to feel like they're all wrong. The subject will feel like they're bad after months of going through all of this, and the guilt will overwhelm them. Upon reaching this point, the agent will begin to lead them to the desired new system of beliefs and identity. The subject will be led to believe that all of the new choices are their own and therefore sticking is more likely. The entire brainwashing process can take several months to even years. It's not something that's going to happen in a conversation and it's not going to be able to happen outside of prison camps and a few isolated cases for the most part.

For the most part, when someone is just trying to persuade them from a new point of view, those who undergo brainwashing did so. For instance, if you're in an argument with a friend and they're convincing you their ideas make sense, you've been through brainwashing technically. It may not be evil, of course, and you could logically think about it all, but you were still convinced to change the beliefs you had before. It is very rare for someone to undergo true brainwashing where they will be replaced by their entire value system. It will usually occur in the process of coming to a new point of view, irrespective of whether or not the tactics used were forcible.

Techniques Used in Brainwashing

The described methods are used for "real brainwashing" and are rarely used. There are many other brainwashing types that actually occur every day. Maybe they don't make you abandon your old identity completely in favor of a new one, but they help to shift your thinking and thoughts about what is going on around you.

Hypnosis is sometimes a form of brainwashing. Basically, hypnosis leads to a high degree of suggestibility. This is often thinly disguised as meditation or relaxation. During the hypnosis process, the agent can suggest things to the individual in the hope that they act or react in some manner. Many people know hypnosis from the stage shows they saw. It is often also used as a means of improving health. Everybody has an innate need to belong to peer pressure. This could be with a specific group, family, friends, and the community. With the tactic of peer pressure, the doubt is eliminated that the subject feels along with the release of its resistance against new ideas by exploiting this strong necessity. If done properly, the subject may be more willing to experiment with new things, less shy about new people, and make new friends easier.

Love Bombing

The feeling of family in people is very strong. This is the group into which you were born and which you supposedly have been around for your life. You know better than anyone, and those who missed such a relationship may find that they feel alone and unwanted. The manipulator can create a sense of the family with love bombing, by means of emotional connection, feeling, sharing, and physical touch. This enables the manipulator and the subject to bind in a family manner, making it easier to trade in the new one's old identity.

Unbending Rules

The manipulator's rules are often strict and will not be modified. These rules make it difficult for the victim to think and act by themselves; instead, they will spend time doing exactly what the manipulator tells them to do. There are many different rules that can fit into this category, such as those for disorientation and regression, all the way to how medicines, bathroom breaks, and food are allowed to be used. These rules are in place to control the victim completely during brainwashing.

Verbal Abuse

Verbal abuse is one of the tactics used in the breakup phase. Often the victim gets desensitized when bombarded constantly with abusive and foul language. Physical abuse can sometimes supplement or replace verbal abuse.

Controlled Approval

The manipulator will work to maintain confusion and vulnerability during the break-up period. One way to do this is by means of controlled approval.

The manipulator will punish and recompense similar actions, in turn, making it difficult for the victim to know right.

Rejecting Old Values

In the end, the subject will denounce the values and beliefs that it once held and begin to accept the manipulator's new way of life.

Confusing Doctrine

This tactic will encourage the blind acceptance of the new identity while rejecting other logic the victim will possess. To do so, the manipulator is given a complex set of lectures on a doctrine that is unintelligible.

Through this process, the subject will learn to blindly believe what the agent says, whether it concerns the doctrine or a new identity that is being created.

Metacommunication

This tactic is used when the manipulator inserts subliminal messages into the victim. This is done when the agent emphasizes certain words or phrases which are essential to the new identity. The phrases and keywords are implanted into confusing lengthy lectures through which the subject is forced to sit.

No Privacy

Privacy is a privilege that many victims will lose until they have become a new identity. This is not only taken as a way of making guilt and misdeeds more visible to the victim, but it also removes the ability of the subject to assess the things that are said logically. If the subject has privacy, they will have time to take the information they received in private and may find that they are untrue or not up to what they already believe. Removing this privacy means that the agent or officer is always around and always leads the victims to a new identity.

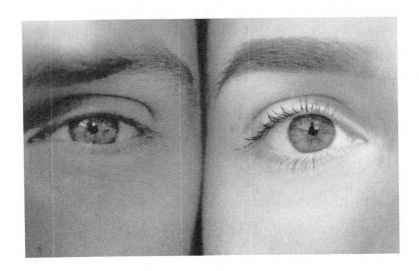

Disinhibition

The manipulator encourages the victim to give childlike obedience during this tactic. This facilitates the manipulator's shaping of the subject's mind.

The Change in Diet

Changing the food consumed by the victim is another tactic that creates disorientation while increasing the sensitivity of the subject to emotional excitement. When the manipulator drastically reduces the food that the victim is allowed to consume, the nervous system of the victim is deprived of the nutrients needed to prosper. In this category, drugs may also be added to the mix.

Games

Games are sometimes used to induce greater group dependency. Games will be introduced, and most of them will be a victim to truly obscure rules. In some cases, the victim is not told about the rules and it must be identified or the rules are constantly changing. This tactic gives the agent more control.

No Questions

The victim is not allowed to ask questions during the brainwashing process. Issues promote individual thinking, which is dangerous for the practice of brainwashing. If no questions are allowed, it helps the agent to accept the new identity automatically from the victim.

Guilt

The victim was told they are bad and all they do is bad. Guilt is a common tactic used by the manipulator to challenge their beliefs and what happens around them. The sins of the former lifestyle of the victim are exaggerated to bring culpability to life and strengthen the need for salvation in the victim. Fear is a powerful motivator and can do much more than the other tactics listed. Manipulators may use fear to maintain the group's desired obedience and loyalty. To do this, the manipulator can threaten the individual's limb, life, or soul for anything against the new identity.

Deprivation of Sleep

If you don't have the sleep you need, you will often be vulnerable and disorientated. This can help to create the ideal environment the manipulator seeks during the brainwashing process breakdown and denomination. Moreover, the victims are often required to do prolonged physical and mental activities in addition to insufficient sleep in order to speed up the process even more.

Dress Codes

Enforcing a dress code further removes the individuality of the victim and the choice they have to pick their own clothing. Often, the victim is asked to wear the dress code held by the rest of the group during the brainwashing process.

Chanting

The agent works towards the elimination of any uncultured ideas in the mind of the victim. One way to do this is by chanting or repeating phrases used by those who follow the new identity.

CHAPTER 5:

Mind Control

M ind control is a term that is used for several psychological phenomena such as coercive control, brainwashing, coercive persuasion, malignant use of group dynamics, and a lot more. It is a psychological theory with many names. The many names given to the theory are a clear indication of the fact that there is a lack of agreement, which makes room for distortion and confusion, especially in the hands of those that intend to make use of it covertly for their selfish interests.

One can, however, agree with the fact that mind control easily falls under the umbrella of influence and persuasion, which deals with the way people change other people's beliefs and behaviors. While some will like to argue that all falls under manipulation, it is important to take note of the missing distinctions in this argument.

It is much better to think of influence as a continuum because at one end there are the ethical and respectful influences that make room for giving respect to an individual in relation to their rights, while at the other end there are destructive influences that rip off a person's independence, identity and their ability to come up with critical and logical thoughts.

When it comes to the darker side of the continuum, we talk about cults and sects. These are the groups of people who make use of deception and mind control skills in taking advantage of their member's strengths and weaknesses in order to satisfy the selfish desires of the cult leaders.

There are one-on-one cults, which are intimate relationships whereby a person manipulates and exploits others using their own influence. These are cultic relationships, which are a smaller version of the larger groups that may prove to be destructive as a result of the fact that all the time and attention available are directed towards a person. These relationships may come in the form of husband/wife, pastor/worshipper, teacher/student, or therapist/client.

The best way to pin a definition to mind control is to look at it from the angle of a system of certain influences that can disrupt a person at their core and at their identity level, which has to do with their preferences, beliefs, behaviors, relationships, decisions and so on.

Mind control creates a new pseudo-identity or pseudo-personality for the person and can be used in several ways to the benefit of others or that of people themselves. For example, mind control can be used for the benefit of addicts and also in bad and unethical ways.

This practice is not uncommon as it is not a mystery or dark art that is known by only a select few. It is merely a combination of words and group pressures that are packaged in a way that makes room for the manipulator to create a sense of dependence on their followers. This helps the followers make personal decisions while thinking that they are independent beings who are free to decide on their own.

When a person becomes a victim of mind control, they are unaware of the influencing process as well as the changes that are taking place within them. First, mind control is a subtle but very insidious process, which means that the individual is largely unaware of the grave effects of the influence that is being imposed on them. This is the reason why they typically make little changes over time with the belief that they are making decisions for themselves when all the decisions that they are making are made for them. It is insidious because the purpose of mind control in some cases is to entrap and cause harm to the victim.

Another distinct point to note is that it is a process that doesn't just happen in an instant. It usually takes a lot of time, which depends on factors like the skills of the manipulator, the methods that the manipulator has decided to make use of, the length of time that the victim was exposed to the techniques, and other personal factors.

However, these days, manipulators do not require a whole year or several months as they have become sufficiently skilled in such a way that they can control a person's mind within a few hours.

Also, there is usually force involved in controlling the minds of others. This may not come in the form of a physical force, but there is certainly some form of psychological and social force/pressure.

CHAPTER 6:

The Three Main Traits of Dark Psychology

D ark psychology is not a single, universally applicable medical diagnosis that can be applied across all cases of deviant personalities.

There are, in fact, a wide variety of ways that dark psychology may manifest itself in someone's psychological and behavioral makeup. There is no absolute division of one deviant personality type from another, and many deviant personalities with prominent features of dark psychology may display elements of more than one manifestation of dark psychology.

It is important to remember that although the internet has spawned a huge growth in problems resulting from dark psychology, these traits have been part of human culture since ancient times. Another, narcissism, takes its name from an ancient mythological character.

Psychopathy

Psychopathy is defined as a mental disorder with several identifying characteristics that include antisocial behavior, amorality, an inability to develop empathy or to establish meaningful personal relationships, extreme egocentricity, and recidivism, with repeated violations resulting from an apparent inability to learn from the consequences of earlier transgressions.

Antisocial behavior, in turn, is defined as behavior based upon a goal of violating formal and informal rules of social conduct through criminal activity or through acts of personal, private protest, or opposition, all of which is directed against other individuals or society in general.

Egocentricity behavior is when the offending person sees themselves as the central focus of the world, or at least of all dominant social and political activity.

Empathy is the ability to view and understand events, thoughts, emotions, and beliefs from the perspective of others, and is considered one of the most important psychological components for establishing successful, ongoing relationships.

Amorality is entirely different from immorality. An immoral act is an act that violates established moral codes. A person who is immoral can be confronted with their actions with the expectation that they will recognize that their actions are offensive from a moral, if not a legal, standpoint. Amorality, on the other hand, represents a psychology that does not recognize that any moral codes exist, or if they do, that they have no value in determining whether or not to act in one way or another.

Thus, someone displaying psychopathy may commit horrendous acts that cause tremendous psychological and physical trauma and not ever understand that what they have done is wrong. Worse still, those who display signs of psychopathy usually worsen over time because they are unable to make the connection between the problems in their lives, in the lives of those in the world around them, and their own harmful and destructive actions.

Machiavellianism

Strictly defined, Machiavellianism is the political philosophy of Niccolo Machiavelli, who lived from 1469 until 1527 in Italy. In contemporary society, Machiavellianism is a term used to describe the popular understanding of people who are perceived as displaying very high political or professional ambitions. In psychology, however, the Machiavellianism scale is used to measure the degree to which people with deviant personalities display manipulative behavior.

Machiavelli wrote The Prince, a political treatise in which he stated that sincerity, honesty, and other virtues were certainly admirable qualities, but that in politics, the capacity to engage in deceit, treachery, and other forms of criminal behavior were acceptable if there were no other means of achieving political aims to protect one's interests. Popular misconceptions reduce this entire philosophy to the view that "the end justifies the means." To be fair, Machiavelli himself insisted that the more important part of this equation was ensuring that the end itself must first be justified. Furthermore, it is better to achieve such ends using means devoid of treachery whenever possible because there is less risk to the interests of the actor. Thus, seeking the most effective means of achieving a political end may not necessarily lead to the most treacherous. In addition, not all political ends that have been justified as worth pursuing must be pursued. In many cases, the mere threat that a certain course of action may be pursued may be enough to achieve that end. In some cases, the treachery may be as mild as making a credible threat to take action that is not really even intended. In contemporary society, many people overlook the fact that Machiavellianism is part of the "Dark Triad" of dark psychology and tacitly approve of the deviant behavior of political and business leaders who are able to amass great power or wealth. However, as a psychological disorder, Machiavellianism is entirely different from a chosen path to political power.

The person displaying Machiavellian personality traits does not consider whether their actions are the most effective means to achieving their goals, whether there are alternatives that do not involve deceit or treachery, or even whether the ultimate result of their actions is worth achieving. The Machiavellian personality is not evidence of a strategic or calculating mind attempting to achieve a worthwhile objective in a contentious environment. Instead, it is always on, whether the situation calls for a cold, calculating, and manipulative approach or not.

For example, we have all called in sick to work when we really just wanted a day off. But for most of us, such conduct is not how we behave normally, and after such acts of dishonesty, many of us feel guilty. Those who display a high degree of Machiavellianism would not just lie when they want a day off; they see lying and dishonesty as the only way to conduct themselves in all situations, regardless of whether doing so results in any benefit.

What's more, because of the degree of social acceptance and tacit approval granted to Machiavellian personalities who successfully attain political power, their presence in society does not receive the kind of negative attention accorded to the other two members of the dark triad—psychopathy, and narcissism.

Narcissism

The term "narcissism" originates from an ancient Greek myth about Narcissus, a young man who saw his reflection in a pool of water and fell in love with the image of himself. In clinical psychology, narcissism as an illness was introduced by Sigmund Freud and has continually been included in official diagnostic manuals as a description of a specific type of psychiatric personality disorder.

In psychology, narcissism is defined as a condition characterized by an exaggerated sense of importance, an excessive need for attention, a lack of empathy, and, as a result, dysfunctional relationships. Commonly, narcissists may outwardly display an extremely high level of confidence, but this façade usually hides a very fragile ego and a high degree of sensitivity to criticism. There is often a large gulf between a narcissist's highly favorable view of themselves, the resulting expectation that others should extend to them favors and special treatment, and the disappointment when the results are quite negative or otherwise different. These problems can affect all areas of the narcissist's life, including personal relationships, professional relationships, and financial matters.

As part of the dark triad, those who exhibit traits resulting from Narcissistic Personality Disorder (NPD) may engage in relationships characterized by a lack of empathy. For example, a narcissist may demand constant comments, attention, and admiration from their partner, but will often appear unable or unwilling to reciprocate by displaying concern or responding to the concerns, thoughts, and feelings of their partner.

Narcissists also display a sense of entitlement and expect excessive reward and recognition, but usually without ever having accomplished or achieved anything that would justify such feelings. There is also a tendency toward excessive criticism of those around them, combined with heightened sensitivity when even the slightest amount of criticism is directed at them.

Thus, while narcissism in popular culture is often used as a pejorative term and an insult aimed at people like actors, models, and other celebrities who display high degrees of self-love and satisfaction, NPD is actually a psychological term that is quite distinct from merely having high self-esteem. The key to understanding this aspect of dark psychology is that the narcissist's image of themselves is often completely and entirely idealized, grandiose, inflated, and cannot be justified with any factual, meaningful accomplishments or capacities that may make such claims believable. As a result of this discord between expectation and reality, the demanding, manipulative, inconsiderate, self-centered, and arrogant behavior of the narcissist can cause problems not only for themselves, but for all of the people in their life.

CHAPTER 7:

How Do You Protect Yourself from the Manipulation Techniques of Dark Psychology?

Understand Your Rights

The main reason that you will feel as if someone is manipulating you is that you will feel as if your rights have been violated. However, you might fail even to realize that someone is manipulating you if you have no idea what fundamental rights you are entitled to. As long as you stick to your lane and do not harm other people or interfere with their lives, you remain on the safe side. Fundamental rights are the acceptable boundaries that define the extent to which one person can affect the life of another. Therefore, one of the most effective ways which can help you to keep manipulators away is to understand where your rights start and end.

Below are some of the common fundamental human rights:

- Everyone has the right to be accorded respect. If you realize that someone is disrespecting you, it might be a sign of manipulation.
- Everyone has the right to determine their priorities. If you decide to prioritize yourself, nobody should try to interfere with that.
- Everyone has the free will to express their wants, opinions, and feelings. As we have already seen, manipulation happens by taking away free will.
- Everyone has the right to refuse something without being made to feel guilty. This is very important because if you realize that you do not want something, saying "No" should be respected.
- Everyone has the right to have opinions that differ from those of others. Disagreements are normal. Therefore, nobody should mistreat you in any way for holding different opinions.
- Everyone has the right to create and live their own healthy and happy life. In short, if anything threatens to take this right away, such as a toxic friendship, you have the right to cut it down.

Finally, and very important to our topic of avoiding manipulation, everyone has the right to protect themselves from being emotionally, physically, or mentally threatened. In the event that you feel this right is being violated, feel free to object, and move away.

Maintain Your Distance

It is easy to detect a manipulator because they tend to change their colors when faced with different situations or when interacting with different people. As humans, we are allowed to adapt to situations and people. However, with toxic people, their variations are extreme. A manipulator can be highly polite when with you, but when they meet someone, they have less regard for, they transform into overly rude or aggressive with them. Similarly, they might seem helpless at one moment but become very controlling in the next. This is a sure red flag that the person is unstable, unreliable and that it will only be a matter of time before they extend the same to you.

The best reaction when you come across such a person is to maintain your healthy distance. A healthy distance means you might not necessarily cut them off completely, but you do not put yourself in situations that might make it easy for them to control you. You should avoid engaging with such a person as much as you can, and only doing it when you need to. We have seen that chronic manipulators do it out of psychological complications, and it might be easier to avoid them than to try to change them. However, this is a personal choice since the person might be an acquaintance who might feel the need to assist them out of their bad habit.

Understand Them

It is very important to understand that manipulation can be a manifestation of a psychological problem. If you understand something, then you can determine how to deal with it. For example, we do not scold babies for soiling their clothes or keeping us awake all night because we know it is beyond their control. As they grow up, these habits improve. In the same way, you should look at a manipulator as someone who is experiencing a problem with themselves. Manipulative people tend to possess low self-esteem, lower willpower, uncertain reasons to live, and an irresistible urge for chaos and drama.

That said, you should not take whatever they do or say offensively. Their way of expression is affected such that it does not go well with normal people. One of the reasons they might tend to control others is that they feel inferior and need to hurt others so they can feel better. Others do not even realize that their actions affect others because they lack empathy. In short, if we understand that manipulation is a form of the disease, then we can take any manipulative approach lightly. In this way, the manipulator does not gain any power or control over us.

Hide Your Weaknesses

One way to enable it to happen is by allowing outsiders to know our weaknesses. A manipulator's agenda is usually to find out the weaknesses of their victims and using them to evoke the feeling of inadequacy, guilt, shame, blame, or weakness. Therefore, not unless it is very necessary, or the person you are opening up to has proven to be real and trustworthy, always keep your weaknesses hidden. The downside to opening up even to real friends is that you never know when the friendship might end. To some extent, sharing our weaknesses is not even necessary. Weaknesses are part of being human, and everyone has a share of the same. Therefore, if you can keep the shortfalls to yourself and feel satisfied with them, it can be the best defense against manipulation. After all, everyone has their flaws, and they do not go around preaching about them. Once the manipulator has no shortcuts to accessing our most powerful emotions, they cannot succeed in invading our lives. In short, know what to share with others and what to keep only between you and yourself.

Do Not Ask for Permission

In our upbringing, we are taught always to ask for things to be done for us. We had to ask for food rather than prepare it ourselves. We also had to require permission before going out or sleeping over at friends' houses. Requesting for a license was meant to keep us in good standing with everyone by avoiding doing what would otherwise offend them. Unfortunately, this training led to conditioning whereby to do something; we need to seek permission or validation even as adults. Manipulators have taken advantage of this kind gesture and turned it into their artillery. They want us to feel tied to imaginary ideals and rules that we must consult with some authority before taking action. Worse still, they install themselves as these authorities, which we must consult.

Honestly, asking for permission, especially to do things in one's personal life is outdated. It is about time we stopped being concerned about the opinions of others about our life decisions. Otherwise, if we need others to approve or disapprove of all our choices, we get cast into an abyss of confinement.

For example, parents should not decide who their children should marry. While this used to be a friendly gesture in the past, things have changed. Arranged marriages risk pitting two people who have no connection together. Such relationships feel like prisons for both partners, and usually, they end in disaster. Therefore, to avoid manipulation of this kind, we should make our decisions without seeking the opinions of others (manipulators).

Ignore Manipulators

If you cannot move away from a person that you already know is manipulative, apply the shield of ignorance. One of the mistakes that we make when dealing with such people is giving them the attention they so much desire. Once they get the attention, they gain the upper hand in initiating the mind poisoning process. Therefore, if you see or suspect that a manipulative person is making moves at you, just ignore them. For instance, if someone is giving too many compliments yet you are not acquainted with them, resort to ignoring them. You can tell them that the compliments are enough and ignore them henceforth.

One risk of ignoring manipulative people is that it might trigger more aggressiveness in them. They are usually fighting with their inner selves and will pour out the anger if they feel they are being ignored. This does not mean that you should not apply ignorance where necessary. On the brighter side, you can ignore them, hoping their human side is still alive. When an average person feels ignored, they pull back and stop their advances. Therefore, assume that this is the response that they will give. If they resort to aggression, you can take appropriate actions such as reporting them. We will go into this point later.

Judge Your Judge

You are the only person in this universe who knows yourself in the best way. Even if scientists studied you for a decade, they would never understand you as much as you know yourself. Do you agree? Well, if you said yes, then learn to trust yourself and stop the narrative of doubting your decisions or instincts. You have learned that a manipulator tries to sow doubt in you through techniques such as crazy making, twisting reality, lying, and gaslighting. If you study these methods well, you will realize they are all pegged on self-doubt. In short, if you trust other people more than you do yourself, it is a recipe for manipulation.

The best way to start trusting in yourself is by taking away the power of others to define you. In this world, everyone you meet has a different opinion about you. Imagine what would happen if you believed everything that everyone you meet said about you. You would not only be confused but also hurt. Therefore, focus on your understanding of yourself and ignore what other people think or say about you. Once you have strong beliefs about yourself, it makes it hard for manipulative people to interfere with you. Your thoughts act as the shield against toxic invasion.

Record Interactions Toxic People

You might have probably started seeing this as a method that is a little overboard, but trust me, it might save you psychological torture. Remember, we said that manipulative people have the habit of saying things and later denying them. They might also say or do bad things to you and later turn the tables so you end up being the bad guy. To overcome such incidences, you can record the interactions with the people you have identified as manipulative. Think about it; if you provided evidence that someone said something while they are at the helm of denying it, you not only shame them but also discourage them from repeating it.

In today's world of smartphones and computers, recording a chat or phone conversation is as easy as pressing a button. You can keep the conversations you have with suspicious people. During something like a call, when the manipulation starts, you can start recording. Even in face-to-face conversations, if someone is trying to blackmail you, you can secretly tap the conversation using your phone or discreet devices. If it ever gets to a point where they start denying saying or doing something, provide the evidence. This is enough to silence them permanently.

CHAPTER 8:

How to Apply "Dark Psychology" Practices in Your Life

P eople use psychology within their daily lives, so why not use dark psychology and the tactics to protect yourself in everyday life. There are quite a few personality traits that can be very harmful if you get caught up in them. Sadists fall under this category. For instance, this personality type enjoys inflicting suffering on others, especially those who are innocent. They will even do this at the risk of costing them something. Those diagnosed as sadists feel that cruelty is a type of pleasure that is exciting and can even be sexually stimulating.

We do have to face the fact that we manipulate people and deceive people all the time. When it comes to deception, people are deceiving others daily, but they are also deceiving themselves. People often lie to gain something or to avoid something. They might not want to be punished for action, or they might want to reach a goal, and they self-deceive to get there.

An example of how people can deceive themselves is having a hard time studying. This is a common occurrence. When people are trying to learn, they find many things that can distract them, especially cell phones and social media apps. They will find just about anything to distract them from the task at hand. These types of people seem to have a phobia of not studying long or well enough. They are afraid that they will come home with a bad grade and show how unintelligent they are. So, they take the art of self-deception and develop the idea that will help prevent them from studying. This excuse will weigh better in their mind if they do end up getting a bad grade on their test. The person's subconscious tells them that it is better for them to get bad rates for lack of studying than to study and to fail and therefore to have to blame their intelligence. They couldn't live with that.

Here are other ways that we regularly deceive ourselves:

- **Procrastinating:** people often waste time when they do not want to study or do something important. However, the main reason for procreating could be the phobia of failing, and procrastinating was just an excuse. Self-confidence can be an issue as well.

- **Drinking, doing drugs, and carrying out bad habits:** people often fall into bad habits, consume, or do drugs just to have something to blame if they lose again. This type of person will try to convince themselves that they could be very successful if they could stop doing drugs when they are the ones deceiving themselves and standing in their way.

- **People often hold back because life is unfair:** they tell themselves that we all live in a big lie that most people believe in, but not them. It is easier to blame it on life being unfair than hold ourselves accountable for not reaching our goals.

If you realize that you have been deceiving yourself, here is a couple of things that you can do to change that:

- Remember that you are smart, and the fact that you have been able to deceive yourself reaffirms it. If you were not wise, there would have been no way that you would have been able to come up with some of those ideas.

- It is important to learn how to face your fears. If you are running from a certain trauma or not wanting to take a test, you must remind yourself that you are stronger than this and beat it.

- Lastly, once you face your fears, your self-confidence and courage will grow.

Manipulation in Our Daily Lives

Manipulation is an underhanded tactic that we are exposed to daily. Manipulators want nothing more than to get their needs met, but they will use shady methods to do so. Those who grew up being manipulated, or being around manipulation, find it hard to determine what is going on. If you are experiencing it again, it might feel familiar. Maybe you were manipulated in a relationship, or the current relationship you are in reminds you of your childhood.

This is important because manipulation tactics break apart communication and break a person's trust. People will often find ways to manipulate the situation and play games rather than speaking honestly about what is going on. However, others value communication only to manipulate the situation to reveal the other person's weaknesses to be in control. These types of people often do this in conversation. They have no concern with listening to others or talk about anything about themselves. And they are not there to help those people get through whatever it is that they are going through. It is all about dominance in this case, and that's it.

Below are some of the tactics that can be used on an everyday basis. Some of the common techniques that we can experience are:

- **Lying:** white lies, untruths, partial or half-truths, exaggerations, and stretching the truth.

- **Love flooding:** through endless compliments, affection, or through what is known as buttering someone up.

- **Love denial:** telling someone that they do not love you and withhold your love or affection from them until you get what you want.

- **Withdrawal:** through avoiding the person altogether or giving them the silent treatment.

- **Choice restriction:** giving people options that distract them from the one you don't want them to make.

- **Reverse psychology:** trying to get a person to do the exact opposite of what you want them to do to motivate them to do the direct opposite, which is what you wanted them to do in the first place.

- **Being condescendingly sarcastic or having a patronizing tone**: to be fair, we are all guilty of doing this once in a while. But those who are manipulating us in conversation are doing this consistently. They mock you; their tone indicates that you are a child, and they belittle you with their words.

- **Speaking in universal statement or generalizations:** the manipulator will take the statement and make it untrue by grossly making it bigger. Generalizations are afforded to those who a part of a group of things. A universal statement is more personal. An example of universal statement is "You always say things like that." And an example of generalization is "Therapists always act like that."

- **Luring and then playing innocent:** we, or someone we know, are good at pushing our loved ones' buttons. However, when a manipulator tries to push their spouse's buttons and then act like they have no idea what happened, they automatically get the reaction they were after. This is when their partner needs to pay close attention to what they are doing. Those who are abusive will keep doing this repeatedly until their spouse will start wondering if they are crazy.

- **Bullying:** this is one of the easiest forms of manipulation to recognize. For example, your spouse asks you to clean the kitchen. You don't want to, but the look they are giving you indicates that you better clean it or else. You tell them sure, but they just used a form of violence to get you to do what they wanted. Later, they could have told you that you could have said no, but you knew you couldn't. It is important to note that if you fear that you cannot say no in your relationship without fearing for your safety, you need to leave the relationship.

- **Using your heart against you:** your spouse finds a stray kitten and wants to bring it home. The logical thing to do would be to discuss being able to house and afford the cat. But instead, they take the manipulative approach. Their ultimate goal is to make you feel bad about not taking care of the animal. Don't let anyone, even your spouse, make you feel that you cannot make the best choice for you. You do not have to take care of the kitten if you don't want to. Bottom line. Meet their manipulations with reasonable alternatives.

- **"If you love me, you will do this":** this one is so hard because it challenges how you feel about your spouse. They ask you to prove your love for them by giving them what they want from you, making you feel guilt and shame. The thing you can do in this instance is to stop it altogether. You can tell your spouse that you love them without having to go to the store. If they wanted you to go, they could just ask.

- **Emotional blackmail:** this is ugly and dangerous. The idea that someone will harm themselves if you leave them is harmful at the core. They are using guilt, fear, and shame to keep having power over you. Remember that no one's total well-being is your responsibility alone. You have to tell yourself not to fall for it. This will always be a manipulation tactic. However, you can tell them that if they feel like they are going to harm themselves, you will call an ambulance to help them.

- **Neediness when it's convenient:** has your spouse started to feel sick or upset when they didn't get what they wanted? This is a direct form of manipulation. For instance, they don't want to go somewhere with you and have a panic attack, that you have to help them through, so that they don't have to go at all. This is not healthy at all, and if this persists, you should think about ending the relationship.

- **They are calm in bad situations:** when someone gets hurt, or their conflict, somebody dies, your spouse always seems to not react with any feeling. They are always calm. This type of manipulation makes you think that perhaps how you are reacting is a bit much. Maybe your emotions are a little bit out of control. This is a controlling mechanism because no one should be able to tell you how to feel. This might seem like they are questioning your mental health and maturity level, and you find yourself looking to them and how to respond in certain situations. If this is something that happens often and you see that you keep falling for it, you might need to go and see a therapist. This way, they can help you work on your emotional responses and find your true feelings again. This manipulation method can be very damaging to your psyche. At the moment, learn to trust your gut. It will not steer you wrong.

- **Everything is a joke:** This is a two-part manipulation tactic. Your spouse will say hurtful things about you, and then when you get upset, they get upset because you can't take a joke. Other times they will joke about you in front of others, and if you don't respond positively, you are again ruining the fun. This is a way to put you down continuously without having to take responsibility for it. Remember that you are not ruining the fun here, but you have to stand up for yourself.

CHAPTER 9:

How to Escape Manipulation

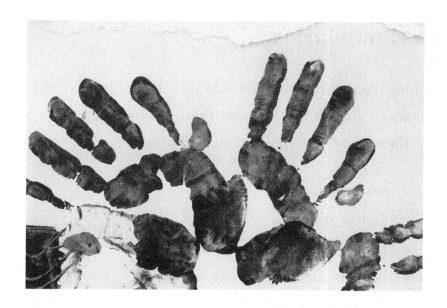

Y ou do not have to be a victim of manipulation. Here are some tips on how you can escape it:

Observe People

Observe people; watch how they act towards others and in various situations. While it is true that everyone has a slight degree of social differentiation, a manipulator tends to be more habitual. They usually act to the extreme, rude to some and overly polite to others—or fiercely aggressive one moment and helpless the next.

When you meet this kind of individual, the best course of action is to stay away from them. Keep your distance unless it is absolutely necessary.

Set Boundaries

Setting boundaries for yourself is a basic defense against would-be manipulators. Know what your basic rights are and use them to set your limits. Your rights include:

- Saying no.
- Setting your own priorities.
- Expressing your own opinions, feelings, and desires.
- Being treated respectfully.
- Protecting yourself.
- Having a healthy and happy life.
- Having a different opinion from others.
- Getting paid what you are owed.

Adhering to these rights will set your boundaries. As long as you are not inflicting harm on others, you have the right to defend and stand up for yourself against anyone.

It Is Not Your Fault

When you feel your answers do not seem to satisfy the manipulator, never blame yourself. Remember that manipulators exploit your weaknesses and use them against you. There is nothing wrong with you; the manipulator aims to make you feel bad and inadequate to gain control and power over you. If this happens, remember your basic rights and ask yourself:

- Is this person treating me with respect?
- Are their demands reasonable?
- Is our relationship one-way or two-way?
- Does this relationship make me feel good?

From these questions, you will be able to determine if the problem is you or the other person.

Counter Their Demands

Manipulators always demand from their victims, and more often than not, the victims give in to these demands. When their demands become too unreasonable for you, counter them with your own requests to see if they know they are demanding too much.

You can throw back some questions to make them aware that their request is putting you at a disadvantage:

- Are you telling me or asking me?
- What do I get if I say yes?
- Does that sound fair to you?
- Do you expect me to do that?

When you ask questions like these, the manipulator may become aware of the inequity of their demands and may stop or back down. However, not everyone will do so, such as the narcissist who will ignore your questions and insist on getting their own way. When you meet this kind of person, use the next tip to stop the discussion and retain control.

I'll Think About It

These words are probably the most powerful words you can utter to counter an unreasonable demand. Manipulators have a way of putting pressure on you to give an immediate answer. When this happens, buy yourself time and distance yourself from their influence. Give yourself power by saying "I will think about it." These words give you the power. You now control the situation; as the manipulator must wait for your answer. This also gives you enough time to weigh up the pros and cons of their demand and consider whether you should negotiate or just say no.

Say No

Saying no is not as easy as it may sound. For some, saying the dreaded two-letter word is uncomfortable; while others may want to say yes but would like to think about it first, others just want to avoid conflict. Saying no is not a sign of rudeness if you say it articulately and diplomatically. You can say no without being rude or impolite.

- If you are saying no, do not feel guilty. You do not owe the one making the request anything.
- They are making the request because they need you and your influence. If you feel that saying yes may violate your boundaries, do not give in. Remember that you have the right to say no without guilt, the right to set your priorities, and the right to live a happy and healthy life.
- Protect your most important resource—time. If saying yes will take up time from your other priorities, be honest. You can say, "I would like to help you but, I have prior commitments."

Take away the sting of your rejection by referring them to someone else who may be able to help them.

Set Consequences

When a manipulator refuses to take no as an answer, set consequences. This would give them pause and could make them change their behavior. For example, "If you continue with this offensive behavior, I will leave (or ask you to leave)."

Stand Up for Your Rights

In tip number two, you learned about your basic rights and how to use them to set boundaries. However, manipulators can also employ bullying through intimidation and physical harm. What you need to remember is that bullies can only bully those they see as weak. Most bullies are cowards inside, and when they see their victim fighting back, they will normally back down. As long as you are not harming other people, there is nothing wrong with standing up for your rights. Manipulation only happens if you allow it.

CHAPTER 10:

Why People Lie

Psychology of Lying

lmost everybody tells a lie once a day or gets lied to. Lying is a part of being a human being with the motive to protect ourselves against certain situations or to praise oneself. The reasons for lying are endless. Can you remember the very first time you realized that you were lying, or you were lied to?

There is a series of ideas as to why people lie, ranging from saving the hurting of oneself or something else, or with the motive to achieve personal gains. However, science has a different perspective on why people tell lies and the different types of lies. Nobody likes to be lied to, and it's not surprising to find that most liars do not like to be considered as liars.

You wouldn't have any trouble in believing anybody in a perfect world, but unfortunately, it's not perfect, so you need to be cautious about whom to believe and who not to. There are professionals primarily in law enforcement that are trained to detect liars. You don't have to have access to the polygraph machines so that you can understand who is lying to you and who is not. There are many behavioral clues that you could use to know who is telling the truth and who is not.

Detecting deceit will give you the rare opportunity to choose your associates wisely without having to say a word. The body goes into an immense ball of anxiety when a person lies. The trained eye will be able to detect these small variances that occur. Although words may speak their version of the truth, the body never lies. Deceit is the act of covering up the way you truly feel through seeking control. Often, that control is executed in a sloppy manner, thus leading to dominant cues that signal deceit. Whether it's a large lie or a little white lie, the results of dishonesty come with a variety of consequences.

Essentially, people lie as a subconscious form of protection. They are either hiding their negative behavior or protecting their reputations. Even when used to exaggerate a story, they may be attempting to protect the fact that their life is truly boring. They want others to find them enjoyable. Thus, various lies are told.

In general, lying requires more cognitive effort rather than telling the truth because you must work harder and strain to make your information or statement sound authentic. After you have settled on the path of lying, you must remember all the facts, but how? You already changed all facts. Having presented you with the small background about detecting lies, the following are now the various ways you could identify a person is lying to you.

Some Liars Are Always Tense and Nervous

It takes a great deal for a liar to pull together fake points to convince you. However, this is not the case with professional liars. These know how to do it just right. But for those who are not used to telling lies, you will quickly notice that their body language is betraying them. On the other hand, a person who tells the truth looks relaxed and happy as far as the story that they are telling is not a sad or painful one.

Some Talk Unusually Slow

If you have ever observed or listened to somebody telling a true story, you might have realized that their speech is normal. However, some liars would tend to take quite long before they can respond so that they have a chance to edit their story.

They act as if they are trying to be consistent and avoid negative comments. But for other people, it might be hard to detect when they are telling lies, especially salespersons; this is because they have recited lines they keep on mentioning every day with their numerous encounters with customers.

You need to keep check of these factors when you are speaking to a person so that you can analyze them and determine when they are telling a lie.

The Hands of a Liar

When people are gesturing and using their hands while telling their stories, this is often seen as a truth-telling sign. However, if the gesturing comes after telling the story, this is often a sign of lying.

The mind is so preoccupied with coming up with a story and realistic details that make sense that the mind is too preoccupied to gesture with their hands at the same time that they are talking. Granted, not all people use their hands when talking, but many people do, and this is a simple tactic that the FBI uses and focuses on determining whether someone is lying.

Breathing

Another good indicator if someone is lying is if their breathing suddenly changes. If you ask someone a question and their breathing changes while answering, this is a good sign that they are lying.

When somebody is lying, their heart rate upsurges and they turn out to be nervous. It makes them breathe quicker and harder.

Too Still

Another good sign that someone is lying is if they are too still. It is normal for us to move around a bit while talking. It could be shifting in our seat or from foot to foot. Glancing around, hand movements, etc. However, when someone is noticeably too still, this can be a sign of deception. People are often aware that their body language can give them away if they are lying. They think that being fidgety and moving around will give them away. Instead, they do the opposite. They focus very hard on remaining very still so as not to seem fidgety. However, this has the opposite effect than what they were thinking.

Gut Instinct

Lastly, but most importantly, follow your gut instinct. It is probably one of the best ways to figure out if someone is lying to you. People are often very distracted when trying to determine if someone is lying because they focus too hard on the little signs that are supposed to tell you if someone is lying. Frequently, just listen to that other person and then ask yourself if you believe them. We instinctually know when something is "off" about someone. Sometimes we can't even accurately explain what it is or why we feel that way, but we know when something is not genuine. It could be the pitch of their voice, their facial expressions, etc.

Watch the Eyelids

If someone closes their eyelids for a long time, it means the person is trying to avoid eye contact.

If the person blinks more than three times, it is a sign of nervousness and apprehension that you will catch on to them.

If someone uses the hands to cover their eyes, this is another sign that they want to "block out" the truth.

Pointing of Eyes

Our eyes point at things we find attractive or where our body wants to go. If you are talking to someone lying, the person will continuously look at the door or watch, signaling the desire to cut short the conversation because they are fearful you will catch the lie.

Avoiding Eye Contact

Breaking eye contact is the most basic way to identify a lie. Someone who has complete confidence about what they are saying will never avoid eye contact.

However, if someone is lying, they will avoid eye contact.

Facial Expressions

Observing facial expressions can help you detect a lie. The most common facial expressions observed in a liar are dilated pupils, the appearance of lines on the forehead, narrowing of the eyebrows, and blinking eyes. Sweat on the forehead and an angry expression are common with these facial expressions.

Dilated Pupils

Pupil dilation indicates tension and concentration. When someone gets worried about exposure, the pupils unconsciously dilate as they think of ways to hide the lie. If you are talking to someone but unsure if the person is honest or not, look at the person's pupils for answers.

Several key facial indicators may tip you off to whether a person is lying to you. Though none of these are necessarily conclusive in and of themselves, learning to notice these indicators will be your ally when determining if someone is less than trustworthy.

Lines on Forehead

Someone lying may have lines on the forehead because of the stress the person has to bear as they seek ways to cover the lie. Apart from the facial expression, we can also observe many other gestures in a liar.

Clearing of Throat

If someone is lying to you, they will probably clear their throat more than once as a nervous tendency to distract from the stress of telling a lie.

Backward Head Movement

When someone is telling a lie, the head could possibly move backward. This gesture occurs as the lying person tries to avoid the source of anxiety because people tend to distance themselves from things they dislike.

Hard Swallowing

The throat of someone who is lying may become dry, and additionally, they may become self-conscious of their swallowing and breathing so as not to give away their deception. Therefore, it is common for a person to swallow hard to bring moisture back to avoid clearing their throat. It is common for people trying to hide a lie.

Statement Analysis to Determine Lie

Analyzing someone's lie through their statement is the last step in lie detection. Sometimes what people say does not support their body language. It allows you to detect lies. People often stammer or talk at a fast pace as a way of trying to avoid discovery. For instance, if you suspect your classmate stole your money and ask them about it, you notice darting eyes and nervousness in their tone. Their body language does not support their statement that they did not steal the money. It means they are lying and have stolen it or knows who did.

No matter how good a person is at lying, if the person's body language is not supportive of their statement, that person is lying. To identify a liar, analyze someone's body language and determine if it matches the person's statement. If the two contradict, you may have a liar on your hands.

You now have a complete idea of analyzing your target by studying body language, expressions, and gestures. It is just one way, however, to analyze people. If you wish to analyze people more efficiently, then you can use the information you gathered from your body language observations. It will give you a complete understanding of your target's state of mind, personality, habits, tendencies, thought patterns, and general operation mode.

CHAPTER 11:

Why I Let Myself
Be Manipulated

Manipulative people tend to disguise their interests as one's interests. In other words, they are the kind of people who will believe that their opinions, as well as facts, are the best and yours don't count. They will attract any form of attention and take credit in places where they don't deserve it. They are the kind of people who will tell everyone how incompetent they are. They will then work on improving your skills so as they can use you to get more credit. If you fail to change the way they want, they will ruin your life. It is worth noting that they are the kind of people who will help you so as they can control you as well.

In other words, they will force you to change not to better your life but so as they can use you. They will do all they can to ensure that they will keep you from outgoing them. They can't allow you to outshine them although they will pretend to be helping you. It is worth noting that once you enable manipulative people in your life, they are tough to get rid of. In other words, they will flip flop issues and make your success path to be slippery and confusing. They are the kind of people who will ensure that they have used all your efforts for their benefits. Thus, it is wise to avoid them and get rid of their schemes and plans. Take a look at some of the techniques you can use to prevent their projects.

Ignore Everything They Do and Say

When you are dealing with manipulative people, one of the biggest mistakes you can do is to correct them. In other words, a manipulative person thinks that their way of doing things in the best, and there is no way it can be changed. They have their tactics that they believe they are the best and all the other people under their custody can't have better ideas than they do. In other words, the art of correcting them should be the aspect you need to avoid. However, what you need to do is to ignore everything they do or say. Also, you should work hard and ensure that they don't realize or understand the things that trigger you most. The aspect is linked to the fact that once they have known the things that trigger you, they will use them to influence all your actions. Uniquely, if they can identify the things you love most, they will use them as a bait to manipulate or somewhat control all your activities. One of the best strategies to avoid the manipulative aspect is to ignore their ideas. What you need to do is to delete all their ideas in your mind. Don't show concerned with what they want you to do.

The aspect is linked to the fact that they will ensure that they have corned you and ensure that they have the credit they want from you. If they happen to be your relatives or your bosses, you may agree with what they say but turn around and do your things. At first, they will be pissed off by your actions and end up ignoring you once they realize that you aren't interested in what they believe. However, if you will accidentally do what they like doing, they will end up manipulating you.

Hit Their Center of Gravity

It is worth noting that manipulative people will always use their strategies to ensure that they are against you. For instance, they may hold past actions over your head and tell your friends to turn against you. They are the kind of people who will become friends with your loved ones so as they can sue them to ill-treat you. They may even get a step further to reward your friends and ensure that they all turn against you. At such moments, they will then pretend to be good friends so as you can tell them all your secrets. They will, in turn, utilize such secrets to ensure that they have controlled all your actions.

The aspect is linked to the fact that if they identify your past mistakes as well as the things you won't like to know by others, you will probably do whatever they ask so as they can instill the secret. The best thing for you to do is to turn the tables and ensure that the deals you have with them turn out to be miserable. If you have an experience with them, you can ignore all their attempts of be-friending you and close all the lope holes where they can understand about your secrets. This is linked to the fact that they will lack a chance of manipulating you. You need to find their center of gravity. In other words, you need to identify the things that cause havoc in them. Pinpoint their strengths and work on reducing them to ashes.

That is to say, if they use words to convince people, ensure that you didn't offer any listening ear to them. Some use parties to influence their victims. Thus, you need to avoid such parties or any offers they give to people so as they can win. Some may have a deeper understanding of a particular aspect of life. Maybe it is a specific resource they control. What you need to do is to avoid all their strategies and ensure that you didn't close their paths. The aspect is critical in the sense that you will be in a good position of avoiding the things that could escalate their manipulative elements in your life. Trust the judgments you make.

What you need to understand is that you are the best and whatever decision you are about to make is yours, and no one can do the best as you do. The aspect is critical in the sense that you will be in a good position to avoid the art of being manipulated. In other words, you will avoid cases where someone is using your capabilities to explore your emotions as well as the things you like. You need to define your life and trust your decisions. You don't have to get approval from people so as you can move on with what you think will work out the best for you. You need to understand that your boundaries are your beliefs. In other words, you need to set your limits and stick to them. The aspect is critical in the sense that it helps an individual to prevent all the manipulative people from affecting their lives. In other words, if you are able to set healthy boundaries, the people who are around won't have a chance to manipulate you. The art is linked to the fact that you won't open up and allow manipulative people to have credit over your efforts.

Try to Fit in

As you cope up or live with manipulative people, you need to keep re-inventing yourself and try as much as possible to fit in. One of the significant characteristics of manipulative people is that they like a situation where you are using all your efforts to please them. For instance, they will love a job where you come and clean their houses and make them happy. They will want a position where you wake up in the morning and prepare their offices for them. They will also prefer a situation where you leave your duties and ensure that they are first fixed. You don't have to meet all their please. However, you can try and fit in their desires but don't allow them to carry you. The aspect is linked to the fact that their ideas are aimed at manipulating you.

Also, if you avoid doing what they want, your life might be miserable. This is due to the fact that most of these manipulative people are your bosses. In other words, they are the kind of people you need to work under so as you can excel. Thus, try and fit in their rules but don't give in to their demands. This means you can look for different ways of fixing their applications rather than using the techniques as well as the strategies they have identified. The aspect is critical in the sense that your actions will act as eye-openers in the desire to change. If you can achieve their demands using other means they may end fearing you because they will understand that they aren't the only people who can come up with such ideas. Thus, they will be cautious in terms of their actions and demands. However, you don't have to show them how sharp you are. They may end up ill-treating you. But, if you are wise in the way you conduct things, they may fear you and avoid cases where they will ill-treat you, because there will be a sense of self-respect that will emerge in between you.

CHAPTER 12:

Gaslighting

G aslighting is a technique in which an individual forces a victim to doubt their existence in order to obtain more control. This happens much more than you would expect. It is a popular tactic among abusers, bullies, cult leaders, and narcissists. Everybody is vulnerable to gas-lighting. It's achieved slowly because the victim doesn't know how deluded they've become, and the individual gaslighting will tell outright lies.

This is an absolute deception, and these individuals are very brazen. One cannot be sure that something they claim is real because they tell lies all the time. The purpose is to make one unsteady and off-kilter. They argue that they've never ever said anything, even if one has proof.

One knows they said something or they were trying to do something, you know for sure you know that. Yet, it is rejected by them, plain and simple. It lets one begin to doubt the reality, and they could never have said the statement. And the more they do so, the more you doubt your truth and continue to embrace theirs. As a weapon, they use what is close and precious to you.

The dark manipulator knows how important one's children are to them and knows one's identity is also important. So maybe it's one of the first aspects that they strike. When one has kids, they advise you should not to have these kids. They're trying to say that you would be a successful citizen if you didn't have a long list of derogatory characteristics. They strike the individual's base. Over time, they convince the other person.

This is one of the subtle aspects concerning gas-lighting; it is achieved over time, steadily. A lie there, a lie here, every now and then a snide statement, and then it begins to speed up. It is so powerful that even the best, most self-aware individuals may be sucked into gas-lighting. That is the example of the "frog in the frying pan," the fire is steadily turned on, but the frog never knows what's happening to it.

Also, their behavior doesn't reflect their words. When interacting with a gas-lighting individual or organization, look at what they do as compared to what they claim. What they say does not mean anything; it's just speaking. The problem is what they are doing.

They put in positive affirmation to mislead one. This person or individual who cuts you down says to you that you have little worth and is now thanking you for everything you have achieved. This gives an extra feeling of discomfort. You say, "Well, they may not be that awful." Indeed, they are. This is a deliberate effort to keep one off-kilter-and to test the truth again. Look at what one is praised for the gaslighter is actually using that to gas-light you.

Gaslighters recognize that individuals like to feel a feeling of security and normalcy. Their aim is to eliminate this and make one doubt everything endlessly. And the normal instinct of people is to look for the individual or organization that will cause them to feel more secure, and that appears to be the gaslighter.

They are substance users or cheaters, too, but they're constantly accusing others of that. This is repeated so much that the other person continues to attempt to protect themselves and are diverted from the actions of the gaslighter itself.

As a last thing, gaslighters are masters at exploiting, and by discovering that the individuals they believe would stick behind them no matter what, and they use these individuals against the victim. They're able to make remarks like, "That person knows that you are not perfect," or "That person knows you are worthless too." It doesn't imply that some individuals really said certain stuff. Bear in mind that a persistent liar is a gaslighter. It makes one feel like they do not know who to believe or turn to when the gaslighter utilizes this technique, and that takes one straight back to the gaslighter. That is just what they want—further power is provided to them by isolation.

How Gas-Lighting Happens

As per the summary report of the National Domestic Abuse Hotline, the tactics a gaslighter could use to exploit someone else can usually involve:

- **Withholding:** which implies that they refuse to listen or they do not understand what they do not want.
- **Countering:** when the abuser makes the victim doubts the recollection of an incident by the gaslight.
- **Blocking or diverting:** this happens when the perpetrator changes the topic or challenges the thinking of the victim.
- **Trivializing:** it happens when the abuser makes the victim feel like their feelings are not valid or insignificant.
- **Forgetting or denial:** this happens when the abuser acts like that, they forget what happened or totally refuse to acknowledge what they said earlier.

~ 93 ~

CHAPTER 13:

Learn to Read People Before They Can Take Advantage of You

The first part of being able to influence and manipulate someone will be when you learn how to read them. You have to get a good analysis on the other person or you are going to end up with a lot of trouble in the process trying to get them to do what you want or wasting time with a strategy that doesn't work for that particular target.

The good news is that there are quite a few steps that you can take to figure out who someone is so that you can learn more about them and pick out the right manipulation technique to get what you want. So, let's dive right into the best steps that anyone can use when learning how to read anyone!

Learning the Baseline of the Target

The first thing that we need to be able to do here is to learn how to get a baseline on the target we wish to work with. The baseline is just going to be when we notice how the person usually behaves when they are not stressed out, overly happy, or have any other reason to act in a different way than what is normal.

While it is common to learn how to watch out for body language to help us know whether the other person likes us or is lying or not, you will find that not everyone will behave in the same manner under those circumstances. When you can take some time to learn the baseline of the target, you will learn how they are going to behave regularly, and then it is easier to catch when there are changes to that behavior.

For example, you may notice that someone is acting a bit jumpy around you and wonder what is going on. For most people, this is a sign that they are anxious or waiting for something to happen. But, when you spend some time learning the other person's baseline, you may notice that they are always jumpy. If that person is usually jumpy, then this kind of jumpiness will not tell you much. But if that person is a jumpy kind of being, and you notice that they suddenly stay still instead of moving around, then this is a sign that there is something up with them.

Each person will be a little bit different from one another, which is why it is so important to start and try to find their baseline rather than assuming that you already know everything about the other person and that they know nothing at all. If you jump to conclusions and don't pay attention to what you can get out of the other person, you will find that it is hard to know when things are normal and off.

Figuring out the baseline of your target is going to be so important to helping you read their body language. Still, it is something that a lot of people are going to miss out on. They need to take some time to practice it long before they even waste their time trying to figure out what one action means over another.

A good way to get some practice is to look for this baseline even before you go out and pick a target to manipulate. The next time you interact in some manner with another person and have a conversation with them, take a moment to notice things like where their hands are, how they are positioning their feet and even the amount they smile. Don't take note or anything because this is going to seem odd, but just get in the habit of being more observant of what is going on around you.

Of course, the more times you can practice this, the easier it is. And once you have that nice baseline down, you will find that it is much easier for you to find a target, pinpoint the baseline that they have, and then you can easily notice the changes to their body language when these come up.

Learn the Different Personality Types

We need to take a look at some of the different personality types that we need to have to help us get to know the target. The truth is, every person you encounter is going to be a little bit different from the others, and this is fine. Learning who they are and why they react to things in a certain way is going to be hard to get each time because all of us are created to be unique and special.

With that said, several personality types are recognized at large, and we all are going to lean closer to one of them or one combination of them than the other. You can use these different types of personalities, and the things that come with them, to help you get a little bit better feel of the target you are trying to analyze.

Here, we are going to take a look at two groups of personalities, which include four sub-sects of personalities within them. You may find that someone fits a little bit of more than one of these, and that is just fine. Learning the basics of them and trying to understand how each one works is not always exact, but it can give you a better idea of the person you are dealing with ahead of time.

The Analysts

First, we have the analysts. These will be the people who like to study things and are going to rely a lot on the facts presented to them. They have emotions, but they are not going to base any decisions they make on these emotions. This means that you should not waste your time with emotional tactics to get them to do what you want. Instead, if you can get them many facts about why they should react one way over another, you are more likely to get the results you want.

There are three types of personalities that tend to fit under the umbrella of the analyst. Some of the personality types that fit in with the analyst will include:

Architect: this kind of person is going to be a thinker who is strategic and imaginative. They like to think things through, and they are going to come up with a plan for everything.

Logician: this will be the kind of person who is an inventor and has an unquenchable thirst for as much knowledge as possible.

Commander: these people like to be the one that is in charge. They are bold and imaginative, and they are going to be strong-willed leaders. They will either find a way or they are going to make their way to get it done.

The Diplomat

Next on the list is going to be the diplomat. These are the people who can think things through in a way that is going to benefit other people and not just themselves. They use logic, but there is often a bit of emotion in the mix. If you want to manipulate this kind of person, you have to be ready to add in some facts coupled with emotion and more. They are an interesting group to work with, and you will find that reading them will give you a lot of the good practice you are looking for. Some of the personality types that are going to fit in with the diplomat are going to include:

The advocate: this person is going to be pretty quiet and mystical, and yet, you will find that they are also very inspiring and tireless idealists.

Mediator: this kind of person is going to be poetic, altruistic, and kind in most situations that come around them. They love it when they can help out with what they see as a good cause.

Protagonist: this kind of person is going to be charismatic and can inspire others when they are the leader. They can mesmerize the people who are listening to them too.

Campaigner: this is going to be a free spirit who is friendly, creative, and enthusiastic. They are really good to be around because they know how to make you smile about anything.

When you find that the person you are reading does not fit into any of the categories above, then maybe they are considered a sentinel. These will be like the guards; the ones who are going to help defend others will help rule and provide counsel when needed. You will find that these kinds of people will be reliable all of the time, making them good friends who can, however, sometimes be more susceptible to the manipulation techniques you use. Some of the examples that are out there for a sentinel personality group include:

Logistician: this kind of person will focus on the facts and think critically about everything. When it comes to their reliability, you can always trust what they are telling you and that they will do what they promise.

The defender: this kind of person is going to be a kind of protector. They are really warm and dedicated to whatever they put their minds to. They will always be there to defend the ones they love the most or those they think they are closest to.

Executive: these people are going to be great at managing things and people, and they are some of the best administrators around, even if you don't want them to manage all of these things.

Consul: the final personality type that fits under this umbrella term will be the consul. This kind of person is going to be very popular, social, and caring. They are always there to help out others, almost to a fault, and you know that they have your back when it is needed.

CHAPTER 14:

Ethical Persuasion

How to Persuade Without Manipulating

Your ability and influence to persuade are determined by how abundantly you place other people's interests first. Successful sales professionals tend not to persuade. Frequently, I am being asked to explain the difference between the two. Aren't persuasion and manipulation the same thing? This may take more in the form of a challenge. Ideally, this happens to be a legitimate question. After all, in both cases, you are attempting to elicit an individual or group to think or do something they aren't going to think or do without your influence, presumably. Persuasion and manipulation could be referred to as cousins, with the view that one is a good cousin and the other is an evil cousin. Ideally, both tend to be based on some ideal principles of the human race, human action, and interactions.

Good persuasion and good manipulators understand these concepts and know how to use them effectively. That's why there may be nothing more dangerous than a bad person with the expertise of good people. Indeed, there are different principles, often the same.

However, the results are as different as day and night. The big difference is the intent. In his wonderful book of 1986, *The Art of Talking So That People Will Listen*, Dr. Paul Swets gave an excellent explanation of both intent and outcome. According to him, manipulation is intended to control, not to cooperate. It results in a situation of win/loss. Persuasion is the reverse. Unlike the manipulator, the persuader tries to boost the other party's self-esteem. The result is that individuals react better because they are treated as individuals who are responsible and self-directed. Also, various intentions and different outcomes are included.

The persuader is intended to serve; the manipulator is intended to damage. If you don't want any harm, don't worry if that happens. Manipulators are so focused on themselves and their self-interest that like any other manipulator, a fully self-serving organism, they only do what they feel is for their benefit, and if someone has to suffer as a result, that's how it should be. What they don't know is that this isn't just a good practice in life. Ideally, this is not a good practice in business.

A manipulator can choose to have employees, but never a team. They may have clients, but rarely get a long-lasting one and a source of referrals. However, once established, the customer base of the manipulator continues to crumble like a stale cookie. They may have relatives and friends, but these relationships are often satisfying or happy.

Indeed, all persuaders and manipulators are conscious of nature. Also, they appear to be the cause of human motivation. However, both use their knowledge to cause a person to take the action they want to take. The major contrast between the two, however, is that while manipulators only use this information for their benefit, the persuader uses it to the advantage of the other person. How deeply you put the interests of other people first determines your power and ability to persuade.

Conclusion

I want to thank you for getting this book and I hope you got everything you could want from it. Whatever your goals may be with understanding and using dark psychology, we hope you found it in these pages.

Remember, dark psychology includes all other criminal and terrible behaviors. Although many are plotting through the discussion of serial killers and psychopaths, a large number of predatory victims are not involved in killings or sexual cruelty.

Many of us struggle in our daily lives. We perform routine tasks to make our lives pleasant and our loved ones happy. There comes a time when we do not always have the energy or inclination to help other people. Most of us will do kindness along the way, though our priorities are always for our loved ones. There is a certain necessity to be strong if you wish to make something of your life. Otherwise, depression can set in and you may drown in the many temptations around you. Excessive eating, or even worse, the temptations of alcohol and drugs could seem an easy way out.

It does take courage to stand up to a controlling manipulative character, but you must be brave and see it through. Push them away from your life and keep them at an arm's length. Don't be taken in by their false promises. If someone encompasses you so tightly that you feel you cannot breathe, then you must escape. A healthy relationship should not feel like that.

This book should enlighten you on how to cope with some of the problems you may face in life. It is meant only as a guide on how to deal with controlling manipulative relationships. It cannot give you your freedom, only courage can do that. Build up your self-confidence. Take care of your health. For the sake of living a happy life, learn how to handle such controlling characters that may pass you by.

If you notice, every one of the examples given here requires you to control your mind and influence yourself using some form of dark psychology tactic. Understanding how the human mind works, understanding how dark psychology tactics can get you what you want, and implementing the tips and tricks given in this book will help you become a better person than before and lead a more fulfilling life than before. So, go ahead and get started learning dark psychology so that you can get what you want in your life.

There is, unfortunately, no certain way to know what another person thinks, and the best thing a person can do is try to take control and understand their thoughts and remain true to what they trust because the heart of the man hides their true purposes.

Whether you are looking for hypnotic secrets, you are looking for ways to be more influential or you think you are being manipulated by someone and want to know how to counteract it, we packed a lot in this book, and know that it can be overwhelming at some points. Now, it is your time to take what you learned and begin to apply it, practice it, and use it in the real world. Whether you hypnotize some friends, have a deeper and more influential conversation with your spouse or significant other through active listening, or simply enjoy knowing that people will not easily manipulate you anymore, keep yourself honed, keep revisiting this book, and do not let the techniques go unused.

At the end of the day, your life is yours to control, and what you make of yourself is up to you. With the NLP and self-hypnosis techniques, you can get over some of the major hurdles that leave others trapped and struggling, and often falling behind their dreams. Your life can be and deserves to be amazing. Whether you use the Swish pattern to make sure that the better life stays in the front of your mind, or you eliminate negative beliefs through reframing and replacing them with positive ones, how you live your life from now on is in your hands.

Be excited. Take action!

Made in the USA
Coppell, TX
24 January 2022

72238696R00066